An Evening with Lucian Freud

by Laura-Jane Foley

Published by Playdead Press 2015

© Laura-Jane Foley 2015

Laura-Jane Foley has asserted her rights under the Copyright, Design and Patents Act, 1988, to be identified as the author of this work.

A CIP catalogue record for this book is available from the British Library.

ISBN 978-1-910067-36-9

Caution
All rights whatsoever in this play are strictly reserved and application for performance should be sought through the author before rehearsals begin. No performance may be given unless a license has been obtained.

This book is sold subject to the condition that it shall not by way of trade or otherwise, be lent, resold, hired out, or otherwise circulated without the publisher's prior consent in any form of binding or cover other than that in which it is published and without a similar condition including this condition being imposed on the subsequent purchaser.

Playdead Press
www.playdeadpress.com

For Mummy

Acknowledgements

With love and thanks to friends, enablers, encouragers and thought-provokers:
Tom Armstrong, Chris Aspinall, The Auerbach family, Rupert Beloff, Cressida Bonas, Christina Foley, Jim Foley, Lucian Freud, David Fulford, Lily German, Russell Grant, Green & Stone, Josephine Hartley, all at the Leicester Square Theatre, Maureen Lipman, John Lloyd Davies and ROH2 at the Royal Opera House, Ella Marchment, Benjamin Ramm, Elliot Robinson, Russell & Chapple, Charles Saatchi, Alastair Stewart, Leila Stocker, Shana Swash, Wonderful Artful Theatre Company and the marvellous creative and technical team.
LF (April 2015)

"The aura given out by a person or object is as much a part of them as their flesh."
Lucian Freud

***

"A story is how we construct our experiences."
Doris Lessing

An Evening with Lucian Freud was first performed at the Leicester Square Theatre Lounge on 19th May 2015 with the following cast:

Laura   Cressida Bonas

VIDEO CAMEOS

Dora Maar   Maureen Lipman
Leigh Bowery   Russell Grant
Model 1   Laura-Jane Foley
Model 2   Shana Swash
Presenter   Alastair Stewart
Lucian Freud   Benjamin Ramm

Laura-Jane Foley is a writer and art historian from London. She lectures in History of Art and Creative Writing at Cambridge University. She has an MA in English and History of Art from Cambridge University, where she also edited the newspaper *Varsity*. She continued her studies in History of Art at Oxford University, reading for a Master of Studies degree, where she also edited *ISIS* magazine. She went on to read for a PhD at Bristol and Kingston Universities. She was awarded her PhD in 2013. The title of her interdisciplinary PhD was: 'Lucian Freud Portraits: Curatorial Ekphrasis in Contemporary British Poetic Practice'. She has worked as a curator on several projects and also assisted Professor Martin Kemp on his blockbuster *Seduced* exhibition at the Barbican in 2007. As a creative writer, her publications include *The Butterfly Book* (2009), *The Old Parsonage* (2010) and her work has appeared in the following anthologies and books: *Cambridge: an 800th Anniversary Portrait* (2008), *Poetry from Art* (2011) and *The Echoing Gallery* (2013). Laura-Jane has also edited Politick! Magazine (from 2008-2010), and written for many national and international newspapers and magazines. In 2010 her work 'Words of Love' was presented at Bradford Playhouse and in 2011 The Royal Opera House invited Laura-Jane to write a short operatic work with leading Portuguese composer Luis Soldado. The resulting work, 'A Far Better Thing' was workshopped at the Jerwood space. Laura-Jane's PhD libretto, 'Sitting for Lucian' also received development support from the Royal Opera House. 'An Evening with Lucian Freud' is her debut West End play.

An Evening with Lucian Freud

The playscript that follows was correct at the time of publication, but may have changed during rehearsals.

CHARACTERS

Laura, an art historian, late twenties/early thirties

Video Cameos:

Lucian Freud, the artist. (His face is never seen)

Model 1, female.

Presenter, male or female; a confident broadcaster.

Dora Maar, Picasso's female muse.

Leigh Bowery, performance artist and Freud's sitter.

Model 2, female.

Setting

A university office.

Note:

The script includes the author's wishes for design directions; these are not prescriptive.

SCENE 1

(On stage there is a filing cabinet, a row of three chairs, a wardrobe that looks like a cupboard, a small table with another chair tucked under, a bookcase filled with books and a number of hanging frames. All of these items are painted white or covered with white paper. It is a blank canvas.)

*(**LAURA** walks on stage carrying a large, heavy black book and a handbag over her shoulder. She is purposeful. She stops centre stage and looks out into the audience. She has arrived at the university research office.)*

Hi. *(A whispery croak. She clears her throat)*

Hi.

I'm Laura.

I'm here for my PhD viva.

I'm a bit early.

(She is awkward and sounds nervous. In this next section it is obvious by her gestures, pauses and responses that she is answering questions)

Shall I just... *(she indicates some chairs to her right)*

Yeah, I'm really nervous.

(She goes over to a chair, sits down and exhales loudly. She puts her handbag and the book; her thesis, down next to her.)

Yeah I suppose, a bit excited. I can't believe it's nearly all finished to be honest. Well, you know, if I pass.

My title was 'Lucian Freud Portraits: The glamorous and the grotesque'.

Yeah, yeah a fascinating subject.

Oh… *(she groans)* I've been practicing my answer to that question – it's normally the first thing they ask isn't it? Why did you choose your topic?' just to ease you in. Or is the first 'how was your journey here today?'

Well… this isn't the answer I'm giving in there. In there it's because 'he's Britain's greatest figurative painter and an academic survey of his work is long overdue' *(this is obviously memorized and trips easily off her tongue – she is no longer nervous)* but the real reason… is because I knew him.

I met him when I was 21. And he was 82 - a year younger than my granddad. I was a student at Cambridge all wide eyed and innocent. Ish. I should have been revising for my art history finals but if you have the chance to meet a modern master you've got to grab it, right? and surely you learn more about art and life from a real live artist than you can ever learn from a book? See how good I was at legitimizing skiving?

(She is no longer having a conversation. There are no more pause/responses)

I was editing my university newspaper at the time.

(sound of typewriters, fast talking, printing sounds)

Late nights, strong coffee, student politics, hacking, politicking, venting, eulogizing. We thought we were so important.

And I thought it would be a nice scoop to feature an interview with Lucian Freud. That's the world famous figurative painter Lucian Freud. That's the notoriously media shy and suspicious Lucian Freud. In a student newspaper. With the immense self-belief that only a 21 year old can truly muster, I made an approach. The internet then wasn't as advanced as it is now so it was a trip to the local library and a look in that big red celebrity bible 'Who's Who'.

(She goes to the bookcase and takes down a big white paper covered book. She rips off the white paper and it's the big red Who's Who book. She lifts Who's Who onto her lap and finds the correct page. As she does this she pauses and looks up and addresses the audience)

Don't get me wrong. We did have the internet. I'm not that old. It's just there wasn't so much of it then. Nowadays you can find everyone's address, phone number online for free 'cos of the electoral roll, company director websites etcetera, etcetera. You can tweet them directly. In those days you had to work a little harder.

Here we go.

Freud. Anthony, Clement, Elisabeth, Lucian.

Lucian Freud.

A big entry.

*(**LAURA** reads quickly through the list)*

(She précis the information) Painter. Married Kathleen Garman. Caroline Blackwood. 2 daughters.

(she looks up directly at the audience)

Mm. And the rest. Educated at Central, Anglian School of Art. Worked on merchant ship. Teacher at the Slade. Exhibitions - everywhere. Works in public collections: everywhere from here to Austra- Ah here it is.

Address: care of Sarah Williams, Williams Stewart, 80 Buckingham Lane, EC7A 5TQ

His lawyer - not a gallery or an agent.

So I wrote to him.

And by return post, a letter with a child like scrawl. Postmark London.

"Dear Laura,

Thank you for your charming letter, which I found last night. I would enjoy meeting you, although an interview would be worthless. After all, you wouldn't interview a horse in the yard. Best to watch it in the field, or stay on and see it in the race!

Lucian Freud"

So I wrote back immediately. I would like to see the horse in the field. Yes please. Thank you very glad. In fact perhaps I could see it at the races? Or take it for a gallop? I certainly piled on the horsey analogies but I forget exactly what was said now.

I wish I'd kept a copy of the letter I sent. But no-one ever does, do they? So when you re-read, days, months, years later, it's only ever one side of the story. One person's tale.

*(**LAURA** writes letter and posts it – either in a letterbox or it flies off in some theatrical trickery way)*

Signed. Sealed. Posted - *(interrupted by phone ringing on stage.* **LAURA** *looks annoyed and when the ringing persists she mouths 'Sorry' to the audience and goes over and answers it.)*

Hello? *(she is annoyed)*

LUCIAN FREUD VOICEOVER:
"Hello? Laura? It's Lucian Freud here. I was wondering if you'd like to come for dinner tomorrow night with myself and Frank Auerbach. I thought you might enjoy yourself".

Oh yes, yes I'd love to. *(Her tone is now obsequious)*

"Do you need to stay – your address is out of London. If you're out of town you can stay in a room here".

Oh I'm ok. I can probably stay with friends.

"Well there's room here if you'd like. Come by at 6. The address is 168 Notting Hill Gate Walk. We'll drive over.

They're in North London. But if you come earlier we can have a drink and a talk…Ok?"

"Ok. Yes, yes. That would be great."

(The phone clears down noisily).

Hello?

Hello?

What's that number? 1471

(She types in 1471 on the phone).

AUTOMATED 'PHONEVOICE- VOICEOVER:
"We do not have the callers number to retu..

(She puts the phone down.)

(She turns and makes wide eyes at audience)

How ex-cit-ing! *(she enunciates each syllable slowly and then squeals)* Tomorrow! Oh God. What am I even doing tomorrow?

Nothing. No. Nothing. (*Phew*). My motto is always say 'yes' and work out 'how' later. Trust me you should follow it. Never say I'll think about it. Or I'll let you know. Cos they might ask someone else instead. Always say yes first.

And so I'm going - to meet Freud - tomorrow. I rush about, getting ready, finding suitable clothes -

(As this is going on, **LAURA** *is flinging open drawers and a cupboard which is actually a wardrobe. It is clear we are now in her bedroom. She puts a number of hangers with clothes on over her neck and sees what the clothes look like in the mirror which is the audience, at the same time she is picking up a laptop and checking online, throwing open a suitcase etc etc. All of these items are colourful so the white set is having colour injected.)*

- working out how to get there, booking train tickets, booking a hotel. *(pauses and looks intently at audience)* I am not staying in his house. Alone. No, no, no. Googling Frank Overbach. Or was it Auerbach. Yes got him. Frank Auerbach. Born 1931. German born British figurative painter. Humph. I haven't heard of him. *(bites lip)* That's bad isn't it? History of art exams in a few weeks time. Useless. Oh God - even more useless as I'm off gallivanting instead of revising.

(as she speaks last lines she finishes packing and zips up her suitcase. She then wheels the case off stage).

(Fade to black)

SCENE 2

(In darkness we hear the sound of knocking on a door. Lights up. **LAURA** *is up stage centre with her back to the audience. She lowers her hand to her side. She has just knocked on the door of Lucian Freud's house. She turns around and addresses the audience. She stands still. The spotlight is on her face.)*

(serious) I arrived far too early. As the minutes crawled painfully by, I skulked around inside and outside the Holland and Barratt shop opposite Freud's house – there's only so long you can spend reading the back of an Oil of Evening Primrose bottle without drawing unnecessary suspicion to yourself - or dying of boredom.

Fin-al-ly. 6pm. At last. I darted across the road and up the few steps to his door. It was a large townhouse - by London standards, surrounded by thick sheaves of bamboo. I knocked on the door and waited. I heard a faint voice muffled through the thick door. And I had my ear up close straining to hear what was being said when suddenly there was the cranking sound of locks being pulled and chains being crossed. He was just behind the door. I held my breath.

And then the door opened very slowly, revealing a slight old man peering around. He was wearing a long coat splattered with paint and he wore a silk neckerchief knotted just here *(she indicates the neck)* Very chichi. He looked just how you'd expect him to look. A stereotypical artist. You couldn't have cast the role any better. He held his arms open for me to embrace him *(she echoes the movement)* and Lucian Freud, the world's greatest living painter welcomed me into his home.

(pause)

(brighter tone now, moving around the stage again)

It was a lovely Georgian townhouse in West London. Just up from Notting Hill Gate. One of those lovely old houses that creak with age. No new floors, plasterboard walls and spotlights. It was largely untouched with all the features intact –the four panel doors, the tiled fireplaces, the original cornicing.

He took me on a tour at first. Up a creaking staircase lined with some of his own very small oil paintings. 'These are for my children; I want to make sure they have something of mine when I'm gone".

(Pause, and then conspiratorially)

Now, there were quite a lot of these paintings. So I think that all the rumours about his vast offspring are proved correct – just by the sheer number of paintings on his landing walls. Well into double figures. As we went around the house, there were plenty of Auerbachs as well. Big bold canvases with inch deep oil paint trowelled on in invariably muddy hues with barely discernible subjects. Freud loved them. Next up were two Cezannes – extremely well executed and well, undeniably Cezanne – that analytical approach to nature, the forms built up through colour. And these were important works not mere studies or preparatory sketches. He pointed out his favourite pieces as we walked around – the walls were crammed with art, this was no white cube.

He was very much a collector as well as an artist. He obviously had a good eye and he told me how he had bought many of the artworks early on in his career at enviably low prices.

(as an aside) I can say this now, as I went past his house recently and saw a major renovation job going on, but you know, when I visited he didn't have a burglar alarm. He didn't even lock the door to his garden when he went out. All these million pound artworks were just ripe for the picking.

He led me through the house, showing me everything. He was very generous and open. Maybe he realized just how fascinating his home and lifestyle were. Even his bathroom: a new one had been installed but whilst the suite was new the walls remained a raw plastered terracotta colour. I suppose he saw it as a functional necessity – no need for decoration or maybe he just preferred it that way. The ripples of dark and light plaster echoed the mould stains growing up the walls of his studio which feature in many of his canvases. Or maybe I'm just reading too much into Freud's aesthetic choices concerning his bathroom installation. On the top floor was a spare bedroom. And hanging on the door was an old army uniform. The very one worn by Andrew Parker Bowles in that famous portrait of a brigadier at rest. It was like *(pause)* a curated gallery space or a film set. All these props laid out as if a bus load of tourists were due to visit. He walked over to the bed, turned sharply around and looked me straight in the face: "This is where you can sleep if you like?"

(pause, she frowns at the audience)

On the way back down he showed me his studio.

SCENE 3

He gestures for me to go inside. I push open the door and take it all in. He doesn't follow as I take a step inside.

*(**LAURA** opens the doors to the wardrobe wide and inside it is revealed to be a scaled down version of the inside of Freud's studio)*

The walls, the floors, the easel, the dangling light bulb, the large shuttered window, the canvases stacked up. Lucian Freud's studio. Close your eyes and picture it.

It is a peculiar sensation to walk around this room. It's almost like walking through his paintings. His canvases made 3D. The familiar props and backgrounds, the metal bed, the discarded white rags on the floor,

*(**LAURA** goes to filing cabinet and takes out very large sheets/rags)*

well, white is stretching it a bit, maybe once they were white. Now more a grey-brown colour.

The paint layered onto the studio wall, thick impasto, multi-coloured oil paint. Pure abstraction; think Jackson Pollock.

*(**LAURA** points to the inside of the wardrobe door and shows the layered up paint. She goes again to the filing cabinet and removes a palette knife, and palette and adds more paint to the wall herself)*

This is years old. He adds to it every day. Loads his paintbrush and smears the excess paint off onto the wall, like a child wiping his nose on his sleeve. An artwork in itself, just there, existing quite apart from his canvases. But there's nothing really here. No representation. No meaning to discern, just trowelled on paint: thick and discarded. Remarkable impasto; it leaps from the wall, on the verge of being a sculpture. It's a masterpiece. An unsellable masterpiece. It means nothing, but signifies everything.

It even features in some of his portraits. The backdrop moves centre stage.

(pause as she puts palette etc down on the table and returns to the wardrobe studio)

You can imagine it so well.

*(**LAURA** picks up the sheets/rags and wraps herself in them)*

The women writhing amongst the sheets, wrapping themselves up, trying to protect their modesty but failing as Freud orders them off.

(she drops the rags and leaves them where they fall on the floor)

Their bodies exposed to his unflinching and critical gaze.

In this studio he scrutinizes them, like a human x ray, he sees the unseen, nothing can be hidden from him. He spends months, sometimes years on end, with his models in this room, staring, looking, gazing, eyeing, analysing. Nothing is hidden from Lucian. Nothing is in this room which doesn't have a purpose. Nothing here distracts him from his purpose.

(A screen flickers on within one of the hanging frames and a video begins playing).

VIDEO CAMEO 1 (Model 1):
"It was a really difficult time. I had to arrive at 7am every morning. Without fail. He hated any changes to his schedule.

He actually forbade me from going on holiday in case I developed a tan. Warned me, in very strong words, not to put any weight on and vetoed any hair style changes. He would scrutinize my appearance each time I arrived, checking for any changes.

I was so uncomfortable but I was too shy and timid to say anything. On that first morning I was moving about trying to twist away from a splintered bit of floorboard when Lucian said 'that's it. That's the pose. Stay like that'. But it was dreadful. I was contorted. Some models talk about falling asleep during sittings. God, if only. It was torture. My left arm, trapped beneath me, would turn a funny shade of purple and then I would lose all feeling in it for about 3 hours. It was an ordeal. A daily ordeal as he endlessly repainted, reworked and scraped off before reloading his palette for the next assault.

It took nine months. From conception to delivery, if you like. He wanted to use me for another painting straight away but I couldn't stand it any longer. I didn't enjoy it like the other girls. Maybe if we'd been sleeping together it would have been different but I was only newly married…

When I looked at myself in his canvas, tears just… I could not understand how he could see me like this. It was brutal. My flesh spilled out onto the sofa, filling the creases and crevices and my face… Was this really who I was? It looked like me but, but, it didn't feel like me. It was like… I don't want to say it, but… it was like he hated me".

(Long pause.)

VOICE OVER:
"Laura" *(voice over distant, repeated a bit louder and then a bit louder again)*

"Laura"

I'm suddenly aware of his voice calling me.

"Laura"

The moment's broken.

VOICE OVER:
"Laura, would you like a drink"

I turn my back on his studio. Reluctantly. And go back downstairs. We have time before we have to head out for dinner.

(Fade to black. The rags are moved to the side.)

SCENE 4

*(***LAURA** *is sat down on a chair next to the small table. The palette is still on the table.)*

He offers me a choice.

Champagne or green tea?

Well, there's only ever one proper answer to that isn't there?

He leaves me alone as he goes down to the cellar to bring up a bottle.

So I have a good shufty around the room. We're in a through living room. At the back a huge Rodin bronze stands atop a round dining table. Beneath it the table overflows with letters and packaging and the detritus of life admin. It's funny to see this million pound work of art not on display but just part of the furniture.

(pause)

I suppose it's a nice way to see a sculpture isn't it? in a home? life existing around it. Rather than in the sterile setting of an art gallery.

I wouldn't mind a Rodin propping up my bank statements and 'phone bills.

Opposite the Rodin there was a kitchen area but it didn't look much used. Paintbrushes lay where me and you might leave our cutlery. There was some food though. Several punnets of strawberries and raspberries were left out on the work surface. Lucian didn't strike me as a particularly domesticated soul. I think his dinners were mostly courtesy of The Wolseley and Sally Clarke's, the restaurant next door but one, where he also went for breakfast most mornings. He always took his sitters out to dinner – he wanted to observe them in every possible setting.

(she is musing and drifting slightly)

Anyway, he reappeared with a bottle of Cristal.

Swanky.

We clink and drink.

He shows me some of his letters and correspondence. He receives an awful lot of it. Some gushing, some mildly deranged, many contain drawings and artworks.

(She unfolds some of the letters and drawings on the stage)

He told me that it was the only way he really met people. Most of the correspondents however, were distinctly odd and he said he rarely replied. Look at this one sending his work.

*(**LAURA** shows a particularly weird one to the audience)*

The letter, full of grossly over the top praise and adoration, is written by a young male artist. One with delusions of grandeur:

"I love your work. It is sublime. It is
better than the Old Masters. I see you as
an older version of myself. I expect you

will see something of yourself in my work. I enclose some drawings for your consideration"

(She holds the artwork up to the audience)

Not good is it? And a slightly mad letter.

As is this one:

"You are my number one choice artist. Please help me become success like you. You only have success because of your family. I have no family to help me. Please help a true artist, like myself to achieve the success also"

Mm. I don't think English is their first language. Well, I hope not. Otherwise, it's just rude.

I'm not sure why they write to him. Why would you send your artwork to another artist? Wouldn't it be better to approach a curator or a collector? Far better for Charles Saatchi to know that you can draw rather than a fellow artist who, let's face it, is a potential rival.

(she shrugs)

"I'm glad you wrote though" he tells me making me blush crimson and avert his gaze.

(Pause)

There is a mildly awkward pause until he asks about my exams and he offers me books about his work. Lots of books. He was very generous. "This is a good one. And this. That's etchings. Must have a copy of this. This one. This is a very good essay. From the Tate retrospective. This accompanies an exhibition of etchings later this year."

He loaded me up. No wonder I wrote my PhD on him. I had a ready made Freud library.

SCENE 5

Despite his obvious pleasure with what was written about him in the books he gave me, in general, Freud wasn't very forthcoming about his art. He hated having to explain what anything meant in his work and resisted the labels art historians and critics attempted to pin on him. Especially anything that attempted to link his lineage to the art he produced.

In the forties he produced a series of artworks which featured a zebras head – one, entitled *The Painter's Room* depicts a red and white striped zebra poking his head through a window into a sparse room containing a couch, a palm tree, a red shawl and a top hat. Now, if the grandson of Sigmund Freud paints a picture depicting a couch and containing such disparate objects it's hard to resist a psychological reading of it– and it's evener harder not to see the image as intensely surreal.

But Lucian was having none of it.

"I'm not a Surrealist", he would protest, "I only paint what's in front of me". And true enough, he did own a stuffed zebra's head.

(She removes a stuffed zebras head, red shawl and top hat from the filing cabinet and lays them at the front of the stage)

I suppose you can't deny his logic.

But he was a difficult man - constantly contradicting himself.

Whilst he didn't do interviews now - that hadn't always been the case.

He was a journalist's nightmare.

VIDEO CAMEO 2 (Interviewer/Freud):
*(a clip begins playing in the frame. It shows a **PRESENTER** interviewing **FREUD** whose face we don't see. **FREUD** answers very slowly and there are pauses in his speech. It is highly awkward. There is freedom to improvise.)*

PRESENTER:
You are one of the world's greatest living painters-

(Freud laughs)

Well you are. Do you dispute this?

(silence)

Your grandfather was of course the psychologist Sigmund Freud, do you feel your art has been influenced by his work?

FREUD:
No, not particularly. No more than the rain outside this morning.

PRESENTER:
But surely that too affects your work. If you got wet and miserable would that not feed into your work?

FREUD:
I don't go out in the rain.

PRESENTER:
That's a good philosophy to have. But just mentioning your grandfather again. Some have argued that your paintings can be read in Freudian terms. Certainly your depictions of your family members have appeared odd to some commentators and critics, can you –

FREUD:
Why odd? I don't see that.

PRESENTER:
Well, you're depicting your own daughters without any clothes on.

FREUD:
Does that shock you?

PRESENTER:
Well, it's unusual.

FREUD:
Only to a prude.

PRESENTER:
I wouldn't say -

FREUD:
I would.

PRESENTER:
You wouldn't say it was unusual to paint your adult daughters naked?

FREUD:
No, they shouldn't be ashamed.

PRESENTER:
It's not a question of being ashamed. More, unusual.

FREUD:
Not to me.

PRESENTER:
Ok, well we can agree to disagree. But, coming back to your grandfather again, or perhaps others, who, or what, do you feel has most influenced your work?

FREUD:
Many elements, naturally.

PRESENTER:
Would you care to elucidate some of those?

FREUD:
No. My work should stand alone.

PRESENTER:
Ok, well -

FREUD:
(*Interrupting*) To represent is to deceive.

It's finished because I say it's finished

(Video screen turns black)

*(***LAURA*** sighs)*

LAURA:
Ay ay ay. That was torturous. So he'd learnt by the time I approached him, not to give interviews. He followed the

royal dictum 'never complain, never explain'. Kate Moss, one of his models, and of course the world famous catwalk model, manages herself in much the same way. Everyone is much more interested in those who keep an element of mystique about themselves. They fascinate by their silence. Freud was the same.

When anyone ever found out I was writing my PhD on him, I would always be asked the same questions. People would go wide eyed and ask in a half whisper:

What was he really like?
Why was he so secretive?
Was it true he had hundreds of love children?

And of course the family name helped his appeal. Freud. Being a Freud can never hurt your chances can it? – whatever field you're in.

Psychoanalysis. Literature. Art. Fashion. Broadcasting. Politics. Marriage even; though Freud wasn't too good at that.

(A growing Freud Family tree is projected onto the backdrop behind - showing Sigmund's descendants and finally Matthew and Emma's marriages to Elizabeth Murdoch and Richard Curtis which appear on the word 'marriage')

What a dynasty.

Freud only married twice. I say only. Most in his generation only did it once. But for a man so associated with affairs of the heart and with such quick changes of heart it seems odd he only took the plunge twice.

He first married at 26 to Kitty Garman. She was the daughter of the sculptor Jacob Epstein. At that time a very influential and successful figure in the British art scene. But she was by no means his first love. He'd previously romanced her aunt Lorna Lee. And he had already taken up with Caroline Blackwood his second wife before his first marriage had ended. And six years later that was it. He didn't try again. His last marriage ended in divorce in 1959.

He was a divorcee living a carefree, bachelor life for the next 52 years.

And carefree it certainly was.

He had 14 children but newspapers are adamant the number is far higher. The tabloids are positively gleeful when they salaciously refer to his "40 rumoured lovechildren".

(she makes speech marks gesture with her fingers)

A lot of his lovers became sitters and a lot of his sitters became lovers. Not all but a lot. He often gifted artist proof etchings to them when the sitting was over. They'd all be personally inscribed. To Binky, or Sue, or whoever, Love from Old Lu. And over time this has become an increasingly generous gift.

Freud etchings now sell at Christies and Sothebys from a minimum of £5000 right up to 150 grand. Nice prezzie. The model in the Benefits Supervisor paintings, sold the etching Freud gave her about a decade ago and now has to clench her teeth and take deep breaths as she sees the prices rise with each auction. There are several etchings depicting her and the last sold for £121,000.

However, at the time, it was just a piece of paper in exchange for all that time they devoted to him. And an artist's proof – not one from the more valuable numbered edition – basically a glorified photocopy.

Freud expected his sitters to spend virtually all of their waking hours with him, sitting for him, dining with him. Freud wanted his paintings to be the person. He had to know them well to do this. Socially, emotionally, physically, intimately. Often biblically.

Women flocked to him, fell at his feet. There's even a painting showing this - a naked young woman on the floor grasping his legs as he stares impassively off canvas.

And they let him treat them, on the whole, so very badly.

But it was their choice. No one forced them. Certainly not Freud. They had to come to him. It was no secret what he was like. But everyone thinks they're special don't they? That they can make someone change. That this time it will be different. That this time he won't leave. This time. This time. With me. But there was always a next time with Freud. Always a new canvas to paint. A new truth to uncover with his brush.

SCENE 6

Anyway, I digress. Let's get back to the story.

Suddenly it was time to go. Dinner was in forty minutes.

(*sounds of traffic noise throughout scene*)

I followed Lucian out of the house, across the road, dangerously darting between cars. We went to a little side street where his vintage roller was parked and clambered in.

(She moves to sit on a chair as if it's a car. Facing forward. Grabbing hold of her handbag on her knee).

And off we went.

(She shunts violently forward)

It was the worse bloody ride of my life.

He drove like a maniac.

Through red lights.

The wrong way down one-way streets.

(She shunts to the side)

Mounting the curb.

Cars beeped.

(she puts her hand to her face)

Drivers swore.

And stuck two fingers up.

Lucian gesticulated back angrily.

I prayed I'd still be alive at the journey's end.

At one point, a skin head clambered out of his van heading for the car.

I smiled meekly trying to diffuse the situation...

(she makes a grimace/smile; an apologetic face)

... which I hoped conveyed: "please don't hurt my dear old granddad or little me". I flicked my hair. My eyelashes. Unfortunately Lucian was also flicking his middle finger.

But the young skin head didn't have a chance. Lucian may have been old but he definitely wasn't slow.

Bang - that was the exhaust on the curb - we were zooming out of there.

He reversed and roared off back down the road and the skin head was well out of sight.

Lucian was now lost and we started going round in circles. Even to non-Londoner me, the streets were beginning to look familiar.

Haven't we already been past that pub before?

Lucian started fumbling in his pocket, looking for a scrap of paper with Frank and Julia's phone number on it.

My eyes were fixed on the road straight ahead.

Lucian!

He peered up and screeched the tyres braking to avoid a young mother pushing a pram across the road.

(She shunts forward again)

He handed me a piece of paper. Now no-one was watching the road. I'd given up. If we hadn't crashed yet we'd probably make it ok.

I phoned on my mobile. Hi. It's Laura. Lucian's erm *(pause)*. I'm with. *(awkward, trying to phrase it correctly)* I'm coming for dinner with Lucian. *(she sighs in relief to audience)* We're a bit lost. Do you think you can help us? Where are we? Err.

Quick drive down there. What road is that?

Fitzroy Road.

Ok. so next left. Great. great.

(ad libs taking directions, instructing Lucian).

Brilliant. Lucian recognizes it now. See you soon. Thank you.

SCENE 7

(**LAURA** *is at the small table. She lays the table with a tablecloth, cutlery etc before sitting down. Classical music plays lightly in the background*)

The dinner itself was a rather homely occasion. We sat around a normal dining table in a fairly modest and normal basement flat in normal North London and Frank Auerbach's very nice and normal wife Julia was a perfect hostess. It was achingly middle class and well, normal. That word again. The clean, crisp tablecloth, the places perfectly set, the cutlery –just so. It didn't feel different, or special, or… I don't mean to sound rude. It was lovely but I think it was just odd that these intense, work consumed artists had such mundane, normal eating arrangements. I don't know what I expected – food slinging? eating out of tins? paint smeared surfaces? eating with fingers maybe? Both artists had, to a degree, opted out of society – spending all day painting is an alternative lifestyle – maybe this was their luxury, their concession to normality. Eating at a table. With a knife and fork and a napkin in their lap.

Like Freud, the Auerbach's also had a lot of art including two Freud etchings; one of Eli the dog which took pride of place near to where we ate and another one entitled 'Susanna'. Which is the one I was given. I'm glad it's one of a clothed woman. I'd hate to have the naked female anatomy, beautiful as it is, sprawled over my walls in all its, not glory, in all its… realness - but then it would be a crime to hide a Freud away. Bit of a toss-up. I wonder what Roman Abramovich does with his huge painting of a naked Sue Tilley? He bought the famous vast, canvas of the naked, reclining overweight benefit's supervisor for £17.2 million pounds in 2008.

Can you imagine it though – greeting your guests in the entrance hall or looming over your bed?

(Laura grimaces at the audience)

Over dinner, the two artists were in reminiscing mode. They talked about their past at art schools as students and teachers. This can't just have been for my benefit. I think they enjoyed talking about the old days. It's comforting to remember, to recite the same lines.

I listened agog to a well rehearsed re-telling of stories and tales. Auerbach recalled being taught at art school by the English artist David Bomberg. He was a dominating and radical figure who believed that paint shouldn't just record what's in front of you but should also embody your emotions and feelings towards what is being painted. Bomberg's approach was a huge influence in Auerbach's work.

Because of this, Auerbach's canvases were far more impressionistic than Freud's – he trowelled the paint on even more thickly, if you can imagine that. So thickly, in fact, that the Tate once had to reinforce a wall in order to hang one of his paint laden canvases.

Auerbach began talking about the sculptor Jacob Epstein but Freud seemed agitated, and dismissive of Epstein's influence. He then leant over and whispered. "It was a bit awkward really, with Epstein, as I was married to his daughter… and then I wasn't".

Freud, keen to move the discussion on, suddenly interjected: "Did I tell you that I met Picasso several times?"

(a video begins playing within the frame)

(train noises in the background)

VIDEO CAMEO 3 (DORA MAAR):
Ah, ah. He's bringing this one up again yah? Have you heard the story of how Lucian travelled with me on the train, huh? You recognize me, yes? Very famous painting. Weeping Woman?

No? Eurgh. Ignoramuses. I'm Dora Maar. Picasso's muse. From me he created a masterpiece. The year is 1948. Freud was entrusted to deliver me to London by train from Brighton for an exhibition. And he unwrapped me on board and sat me in the seat opposite and spent the entire journey staring at me. Studying every inch of me. Examining me. Eyeballing me till one of us broke. But I didn't break. I stared right back. Like I am right now.

Yes, not blinking.

Picasso thought he was a tosspot. A young pretender. Freud came over and visited him in his studio in Paris. He brought several paintings with him. What is it with these young painters? Why do they think an old master like the maestro Picasso would care about the paltry work they are producing?

Oh the arrogance of youth. Gah.

Incroyable.

(Screen turns black)

LAURA:
After pudding and coffee, Lucian said it was time to leave. Frank's wife Julia was a mass of motherly and caring concerns regarding our road traffic safety. But Freud shrugged off our earlier problems and herded me out.

And as we walked to the car, he stopped and said forlornly, with large puppy dog eyes: "you won't go though will you? We can have another drink?"

Oh yes, definitely, I like late nights!

SCENE 8

We didn't go straight home. We went via Marble Arch where Freud mounted the curb outside the tube and "parked"

*(***LAURA** *makes speech mark gesture again)*

and leapt out to buy the next day's papers from a newspaper seller. I thought this was very cool. Where I came from, the first edition was the only edition and it was available from the newsagents at 8am, if you're lucky, on the day. You certainly couldn't buy it the night before.

Lucian was keen to get the papers as he thought he might be mentioned in them. When we got back to Notting Hill, he spread them all over the table, filleted them – money, sport, travel out - and began to scan the articles for mention of his name. It was a strangely intimate, domestic scene. Lucian and I sat reading the papers over the dining table; the silence punctuated by him reading bits out to me that interested or tickled him.

And at some point another bottle of Cristal emerged.

When he did finally find a mention of himself he criticized the writer. "She's stupid. She doesn't know what she's talking about", he said when he found a reference to the documentary that had just been made about him by Frank Auerbach's son.

As Freud sat reading the newspapers, I was transfixed – immobilized not just by the effects of the new bottle of champagne – but also by the painting propped up by the door. It was quite atypical of Freud's work but was still recognizably by his hand. It wasn't immediately clear if it was finished or not. Whilst the face and body of the naked female was well executed, she seemed to float in white space. It was a striking painting and I felt overwhelmed by a sensation of... almost... wanting to possess it, to steal it. A compulsion. I just wanted to... to... almost become the painting.

I was suddenly aware of Freud staring at me staring at the painting. I turned and smiled. Freud had thought the painting was finished and had sent it to his dealer. But once it had left his studio he changed his mind and requested it back. It wasn't finished after all. He intended to work into it some more but wasn't sure how. That's why he had left it propped up by the door. So he could keep staring at it just as I had been.

But who was she? The girl depicted. I wanted to know everything about her. But Freud was coy. It wasn't important.

I asked him how he found his models and he told me how he sometimes used family. They were used to it and he found them to be a ready source of sitters. He wasn't sure they always liked it – but they didn't complain. And then, there were the others, the sitters who just fell into his gaze. He said he was lucky like that.

VIDEO CAMEO 4 (Model 2):
Well, it was quite different to my normal life, I can tell you. I don't mix with those kinds of people normally. Well that's not true, I do. I know lots of artists and musicians, arty types. But Lucian was a bit more than that. Quite well to do, you know. Posh. And certainly most of his mates or, what do they call 'em, acquaintances, were posh.

But he was a right laugh was Lucian. So many stories, oh he made me laugh so much.

I met him through my friend who was posing for him at the time. And I thought, you know, yeah I could do that too. Bloody hell though, it looked a lot easier than it was. The thing is, everything took so long. I didn't realize when I started how much I'd be giving up!

I was a night picture. Lucian would have a few paintings on the go at the same time. 2 days and 2 nights and he'd alternate. So cos it was night he had this massive lamp with like, I don't know, a 500 watt bulb or something what lit up the space. It was just incredible. But everything had to re-positioned cos the day painting would have messed it up and moved everything about. So what happened right is that he marked it all out in chalk, around the chair, the feet. He'd mark them; the casters in chalk so we'd know where I was sat the last time. So the light and shadow was the same.

But they were really hard to find. Each time I came round, we'd have to search for the chalk marks, sometimes on our hands and knees. Oh, but it was great, great.

It looks nothing bloody like me though. He took so long laboring over me and yet the finished painting has nothing of me in it! I think anyway. But I suppose you, the viewers are the judge of that. But you don't know me as well as I do. But, anyway, it was great experience. Really brilliant. And that's what life's about isn't it? Brilliant experiences.

(Screen turns black)

LAURA:
(ad libs, she's about to speak but is interrupted by Leigh Bowery)

(a video begins playing within the frame)

VIDEO CAMEO 5 (LEIGH BOWERY):
(Leigh Bowery is outrageous - in the way he speaks, dresses and in his gestures)

(he coughs/ clears his throat for attention)

Excuse me. Hello. Looking fabulous over here. All I'm seeing is women! How could you dare to miss me. I think you'll find dear that Freud had a male muse. Moi!

Old Lu had me standing erect in his studio, sprawled missionary style on the floor, lying on the bed, plus ca change. He liked to experiment with positions did Freud – the old dog.

I'm not sure whether he intended for me to be naked at the beginning – I just stripped off on that first sitting – so I was always naked after that.

He was such a blast. Very good company. Lots of tales. Ask him about our night in Raffles.

Many, and I'm being serious here, considered me his greatest work – I am big headed, but it's true - I was his only muse for a period. We had a real connection. But then I introduced him to my friend Sue from the Benefits Office. Boy – did he love painting Sue? Some of his paintings of her are more like landscapes than portraits.

Lots of undulating hills and valleys... and mounds, the occasional bush.

I haven't had a big painting sell at auction so I don't know who commands a better price – I'd think it would be me though. I'm ever hopeful that some rich bitch from Mayfair will put me up for sale! And then you watch the bidders go crazy! Who wouldn't want my dick at face level on the wall of their dining room?

(Screen turns black)

LAURA:
Leigh Bowery and Freud shared an obsession with exploring the physicality of the human body. As a performance artist, Bowery was used to elaborate costumes and extravagant gestures, but for his sittings, he stripped himself bare, even shaving his entire body – a totally contrasting artistic flourish to that which had made him famous.

But, unlike most of Freud's previous sitters, Bowery viewed the production of the artwork as a collaboration, where he was as much involved as Freud. The paintings were just another way of Bowery presenting himself. At last, in Bowery, this powerful nude, Freud had not only discovered a muse, but also, he had finally met his match.

It was now ten years since Bowery had died and Lucian spoke fondly of Leigh, of how they had cavorted wildly around nightclubs and impressed each other with their outlandish stories. Some of which, Lucian was now telling me. Slanderous stories and tall tales of horse racing and gambling, of police run-ins and friendships with cons, of fallings out with artists, of having no money and now having too much money and all the while he is refilling my champagne glass. After one salacious story ends about the actress Anna Massey, the space between the one that passed and the next grows unexpectedly wide and Lucian falls uncharacteristically quiet. I have become the focus of that famous exacting gaze.

He leans over and runs the back of his hand along the side of my face until it rests under my chin. He tilts it up and moves his face in front of mine. My heart is beating so fast.

Out of trepidation, not romance.

(She pauses with her head tilted upwards.)

(She exhales loudly and drops the pose)

He stands up suddenly and moves behind me and starts smoothing down my hair. Then he starts running his fingers through it and massaging my scalp. He bends down to my side and I feel his breath ripple across my hair and his lips glance the top of my ear. And he whispers seductively:

'I'm looking for a new model for a nude'

(Laura drops her glass to the floor)

SCENE 9

(*The moment is broken*)

Oh, sorry. Sorry. What a mess.

(**LAURA** *clears the debris away as she speaks the next lines*)

It's interesting that he called it a nude because, of course, what he really meant was 'naked portrait'. That's what he named them. Freud only painted one nude – and who sat for that? Leigh Bowery. A man. The naked female body – the most consistent trope of aesthetic beauty in the Western world – and Freud can't resist the urge to challenge it.

So a man is his nude – but one who is hairless, over-weight, untoned, rounded, it's not a typical image of a man – hardly a Mapplethorpe nude. Rather, Freud subverts the tradition of nude painting by feminizing the male form.

Sorry, I slipped into lecturing mode then.

Just as I began writing up my PhD Lucian died. His work had slowed in his last years and his palette became quite muted; his last canvas, an unfinished portrait of his assistant David and his dog, was really just shades of white and grey. This colourful, vibrant, intense man just slipped gradually away.

(*pause*)

As we all do. But I suppose the difference is that a great body of his art will always remain. He created work so powerfully resonant that it pulsates with life and because of that and how he lived and how he painted, a part of him will always remain. There's something compelling about that, don't you think? That wish to leave something behind; to create art out of the impressions of life. And for it to last and last.

(*pause*)

Well… (*pause sigh*)

that was the long answer. Probably the very long answer.

UNIVERSITY OFFICIAL (*off stage*):
Laura, your examiners are ready for you now.

LAURA:
Oh. Already. That was good timing. Ok. Here we go. Well, wish me luck.

(*she exits the stage, clutching her thesis*)

(*the stage is left cluttered and colourful, very different from the beginning of the play*)